fast
fun &
easy
FABRIC BOXES

Linda Johansen

C&T PUBLISHING

Text © 2004 Linda Johansen

Artwork © 2004 C&T Publishing, Inc.

Publisher: Amy Marson

Editorial Director: Gailen Runge

Acquisitions Editor: Jan Grigsby

Editor: Cyndy Lyle Rymer

Technical Editors: Gailen Runge, Carolyn Aune

Copyeditor/Proofreader: Wordfirm

Cover Designer: Kristen Yenche

Book Designer: Kristy Konitzer

Page Layout: Happenstance Type-O-Rama

Illustrator: Tim Manibusan

Production Assistant: Matthew Allen

Photography: Diane Pedersen and Luke Mulks unless otherwise noted

Published by C&T Publishing, Inc., P.O. Box 1456, Lafayette, California, 94549

Cover boxes made by Linda Johansen and Alex Vincent

Library of Congress Cataloging-in-Publication Data

Johansen, Linda.
  Fast, fun & easy fabric boxes / Linda Johansen.
    p. cm.
  ISBN 1-57120-285-4 (paper trade)
  1. Box making. 2. Ornamental boxes. 3. Textile fabrics. I. Title: Fast, fun and easy fabric boxes. II. Title.

  TT870.5.J64 2004
  746—dc22

2004010788

Printed in China

10 9 8 7 6 5 4 3 2

Acknowledgments

Jay Thatcher, always

Jay and Janelle Johansen and Evan Thatcher for the joys you bring me

Holly Halley and Gordon Halley, for giving me life & love

Shady & Mocha, still with me all day, every day

Sidnee Snell, Libby Ankarberg, Kim Campbell & Alex Vincent for support beyond the call of friendship. Their busy fingers and brilliant brains are the golden lining of this book. Look for their contributions throughout the book.

Jan Andrews, Wendy Yoder Holub, Nena Bement, Kerry McFall & Donna Beverly for helping to make life fun

Quilt shop owners and their staff everywhere, especially those at Quiltwork Patches, A Common Thread, and BJ's Quilt Basket; these folks make it happen for all of us

The wonderful folks at C&T Publishing; always there and warmly helpful, especially Cyndy Rymer, Gailen Runge, Luke Mulks & Diane Pedersen for working so hard with me

Students and teachers, who took the bowls and ran. I can't wait to see where you go with boxes!

Thank you all so very much.

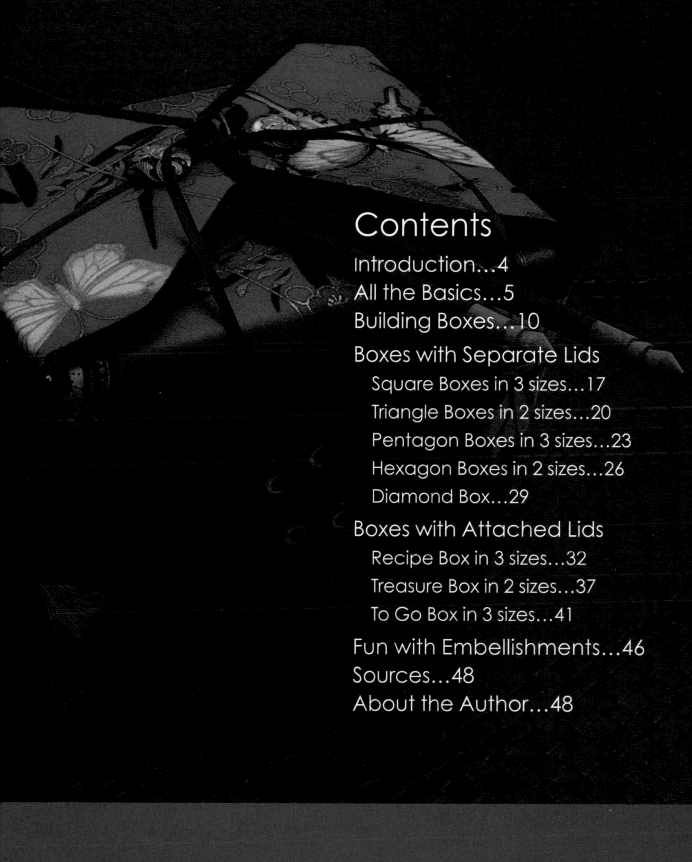

Contents

Introduction

I was either born with, or trained to, an insatiable curiosity. I was also raised to be a homemaker. I learned to cook from scratch, sew just about anything that could be made from fabric, plant flower and vegetable gardens, train and take care of animals, and not much about cleaning house! I guess Mom didn't like it any more than I do.

She also gave me an early art education. I played with crayons, not by coloring with them, but by grating them and putting them between sheets of wax paper and ironing them. We dried flowers and leaves for gift cards and ironed them between wax paper, as well. She made finger paints from scratch and found the paper to paint on. She started me sewing at age seven, as soon as I could work our treadle sewing machine.

I started making fabric bowls after seeing a student slide of one during a class. I have had so much fun with the instant gratification of the bowls, as well as the artistic side of combining fabrics and threads and shaping a bowl to fit my mood at the time. I use them throughout my house as wall art and functional art on the tables and counters, holding treasures, candles, food.

It has been a natural progression in play to leap from fabric bowls to fabric boxes. Just seeing leftover food in a paper take-out box was enough to get me started on To Go boxes! Plus, the boxes are so easy that you can make a couple in a day and still have time to "really" quilt!

With the boxes, you will find more ways to stretch yourself creatively, and more ideas for using up stiff interfacing scraps. You will be inspired to invent and make fabric containers for a long time.

There are as many ways to make the boxes as there are people to make them. I encourage you to play with the patterns, look at the variations, and make the size and shape unique to you. Embellish it to your taste, but most important, HAVE FUN. I firmly believe that fast, fun, and easy can be as beautiful and striking as long, difficult, and complex. Some even call me the "Queen of Quick and Dirty—I mean—Easy."

I don't expect you to always follow the directions. I often call them "insurrections and destructions"! They are here as guidelines, and to help you make that first box or three to see how it all works. You can mix and match techniques in the book however you like. I am still playing too, and who knows what you will turn up next—I'd love to see photos!

Read through All the Basics to get an overview of the materials and techniques. The easiest way to start your boxing career is to make a 4″ square box with a lid. Follow the directions in Building Boxes (page 10), then follow your muse. As always, there are no rules! It is YOUR box.

Some of the boxes can be reversed, but it is easier at the start to choose one side of the box side to show off and put your energy into that.

Choose fabrics and threads that speak to you or mean something to the recipient of the container. Remember, the best gift to give is one you really want to keep.

Happy Boxing!

Linda Johansen

all the Basics

Basic Materials
Fabric

Start with a good-quality, 100% cotton fabric. As you become more experienced with the boxes, play with other fabrics. If you are using a directional fabric or fussy cutting to highlight a motif, you may need to cut larger pieces.

Pick your fabric and thread combinations to match your mood.

Stiff Interfacing

The boxes are made by fusing stiff interfacing between two pieces of fabric. You can experiment with different options to find the look and feel you want for your boxes. The idea is that you want the material to be light, to hold its shape, to be able to take the heat of an iron, and to be washable. The instructions in the book were designed to be used with 22"-wide interfacing.

One option is Timtex, a stiff interfacing developed for making Irish step-dancing costumes. You can also try a double layer of even-weave fabric designed for needlepoint or a double layer of stiff canvas (fuse the layers together with fusible web). You can also fuse together two layers of the heavy-weight fusible web used to make window shades.

Fast2Fuse™ Interfacing (see sources, page 48) has the stiff, light, and washable qualities of Timtex but is already prepared with fusible web on both sides. This is a terrific product that can save time in handling the fusible. When following the box-building instructions, don't purchase the full amount of fusible web—you can use scraps of fusible web to fill in the box corners where needed.

Threads

You can use any thread you are comfortable with for the boxes. However, if this is your first foray into lots of satin stitching, I recommend using either cotton or polyester thread. The needle can get warm with so much stitching, and I have a harder time with rayon threads breaking. When I really want a shiny look, I either slow down quite a bit, or reach for the Isacord (polyester) thread.

If I am having trouble with my threads, I go through these steps:

1. Rethread the top thread.

2. Rethread the bobbin thread, and be sure the bobbin is inserted all the way. If your bobbin has a finger with a hole in the end, try threading through the hole.

3. Change the needle; be sure it's a topstitch needle.

4. Lower the tension on the top thread.

5. If the thread still isn't doing what I want, I change to a different thread. I don't want to spend my time fighting thread. I typically use the same color thread in the top and bobbin for each box; that way I don't have to be quite as precise with my tension.

Fusible Web

Fusible web is the magic glue that holds it all together. I prefer Pellon Wonder Under. You can use any fusible that holds the layers together permanently and easily. Heavyweight fusibles may be difficult to sew and may gum up the needle. Remember to match the weight of fusible to the

weight of your fabric. I am told there is a wonderful rayon fusible interfacing that can make silk easy to work with. You would fuse the interfacing onto the silk, then use the fusible web to attach it to the stiff interfacing. Play around. I fused a heavy silk directly onto stiff interfacing. Remember, no rules!

Note: The amount of fusible web you need for the projects is calculated based on the 18″-wide yardage.

Cording

Cording around the edge of the boxes makes it easier for the satin stitch to cover the edge nicely, takes care of most of those pesky little threads that want to show through, and strengthens the edge of the box.

You can use a $\frac{1}{16}$ polyester cording, a lightweight cotton knitting yarn, size 3 Coats & Clark's Speed Cro-Sheen, household string, or whatever you find that works for you. Keep in mind you don't want something with a lot of fuzzy fibers—that's what you're trying to avoid!

Use a length of cording to make your edges finish easier.

Basic Supplies
Sewing Machine

Your sewing machine should be in good working order, and be able to do a neat straight stitch, and a good, tight (short stitch length) zigzag stitch (satin stitch). A mending stitch (multiple-stitch zigzag) is very useful for joining pieces. Having an open-arm machine makes box construction easier. That's all you'll need for any of the boxes!

Sewing Machine Needles

You need a sharp needle for sewing through the fabrics, fusible web, and stiff interfacing. Size 80/12 or 90/14 topstitch needles work best for me. They have a wider hole and deeper slot up the back to protect the thread as it goes through the fabrics.

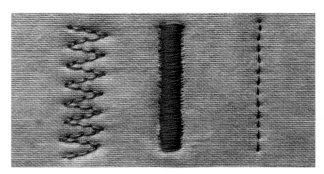

A mending stitch is helpful. Satin stitches should be tight. Straight stitches should be…straight!

Sewing Machine Feet

An open-toed embroidery foot allows you to see *exactly* where the needle is. I use it for almost all my sewing.

A darning foot can be used for decorative stitching on the boxes before the corners are sewn.

The cording foot helps keep your fabric flat as you are sewing the cording onto the edge of the To Go boxes, while an overcasting foot keeps the edge from rolling when you sew the second time around with a satin stitch. Remember to slip the thread off the guide when you go around a corner.

Stiletto

I am a big believer in a good stiletto. Mine has helped me negotiate a tricky corner, get that last naughty little thread caught in the satin stitching, hold down the edge of fabric that didn't quite get fused enough, and many more neat feats. I like

unusual stilettos, such as porcupine quills and bent ones that have an angle to the needle part.

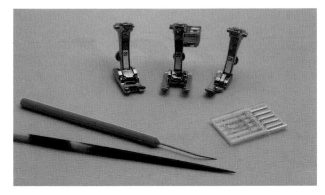

As with most projects, the right tool can make the job much easier.

Scissors

I keep three pairs of scissors handy for working at the machine. This may seem like a lot, but having the best tool for the job can really save time and frustration.

Pair one is a short, thread-snipping pair. Pair two is a 6″ to 7″ pair of good fabric shears for cutting darts or stray pieces of fabric. Pair three has a great long name: double-curved duck-bill embroidery scissors. These are wonderful for cutting close to the threads on the boxes, and trimming close to the stiff interfacing when needed.

Fabric shears, thread snippers, double-curved duck-bill embroidery scissors all come in handy.

fast!

Good tools will make your projects easier and more fun. Go ahead and invest in them; they're worth the money.

Miscellaneous Cutting Equipment

Rotary Cutters: I keep one each of three sizes handy. I primarily use a small cutter for cutting stiff interfacing and the larger (60mm) for layers of fabric and fusible web. (The middle size is great for when I can't reach the other two.) If you are pressing firmly and still need to cut a line twice, it's time for a new blade—no matter how long the current one has been in.

Rotary Rulers:

☐ A 1″ × 12″ ruler is handy for trimming the edges of boxes and lids.

☐ A 24″ long ruler is good for cutting strips of stiff interfacing when you need several same-sized squares.

☐ I use an 8″ bias square ruler for cutting individual stiff interfacing squares.

☐ A 12½″ or 15″ square makes trimming the box shapes very easy for the larger square boxes.

☐ You need an equilateral triangle ruler for cutting the box base and lid base for the triangle box. This must have a 60° angle. I like the Clear View ruler.

Rotary Cutting Mats: At home I use 2 mats 24″ × 36″ side by side. For classes I like the 18″ × 24″ mats. Use the largest you can afford.

Pressing Supplies

Iron: You need an iron with a steam feature that can be turned off, no matter what temperature you set the iron. I buy the cheapest and lightest that let's me turn the steam off. I drop irons. It is just as easy to drop a $200 iron, but a lot easier to replace a $30 one.

Ironing Board: Set your ironing board to a height that is comfortable for standing. Your body needs to move frequently, and having to stand up for short periods to iron is a good thing.

Pressing Sheets: A protective pressing sheet keeps your ironing board free of stray fusible web that might adhere to the outside of your box. Keep the protective sheet *under* the fabric and fusible. I prefer the 18″ square sheets by June Tailor that look like opaque plastic. They don't get as hot as the Teflon-style ones.

fast!

It pays to put a piece of scrap fabric over your entire ironing board in addition to the protective sheet.

Iron Cleaner: There are several brands of iron cleaner, and they all work wonderfully for cleaning melted fusible off your iron. This *will* happen, so be prepared. Follow the manufacturer's instructions for the best results.

Marking Tools

Pens: You will need to mark the stiff interfacing and cover glitches in your satin stitching. I use a standard pencil or pen (or whatever is handy) to mark the stiff interfacing. Take care when marking a light-colored piece of fabric. Colored markers (Fabrico, Sharpies, whatever works and doesn't damage your fabric or thread) are for coloring that last little bit of thread that won't go away even after you have sewn two times around the edge, or for that spot where the satin stitching didn't quite get close enough.

Templates: Some of the boxes call for templates. You can use template plastic, or trace the templates on freezer paper and iron it directly to the stiff interfacing to cut out the pieces.

Basic Techniques

Marking

Use anything to mark on the stiff interfacing that you can see, but use products that will *not* show through the fabric you will be fusing on top.

Pressing

Steam press the stiff interfacing so it lays perfectly flat before you begin sewing.

Fusing

Begin ironing the fusible web to the fabric from the center of the project out to the edges. I use a cotton setting on the iron and press just enough so the fusing doesn't come off with the paper. Smooth the fabric with your hands, and iron from the center out to the edges when fusing the fabric to the stiff interfacing.

easy!

Iron the fusible web to the fabric with the paper side up so you can tell when it fuses.

Stitching

You will be doing mostly straight stitching on the boxes for the corners, satin stitching for the edges (width set at about 4 and length set the shortest you can get and still have the feed dogs move the piece), and zigzag stitching to attach the cording. Be sure to adjust your machine tensions as necessary for a good stitch.

Remember to lock your satin stitching at the end with a few very-short-length straight stitches right alongside the satin stitching.

easy!

Before sewing your project, make samples on scraps of the stitches you'll use.

Sewing the Cording

1. Place the cording right next to the edge of your project under the presser foot. Hold the end of the cording as you sew a few zigzag stitches in place to secure the end.

2. Use a zigzag stitch to attach the cording around the edge of your project. Turn to page 13 (Step 6) for a photo of sewing the cording on.

3. Make sure your zigzag stitch is wide enough to cover the cording and catch the edge of the project.

4. Trim the starting end of the cording before you sew all the way around. Clip it as close to the first few stitches as possible.

5. Zigzag right up to the starting stitches and make a few stitches in place next to the first stitches. Trim the cording flush with the beginning.

6. Satin stitch over the first line of stitches, using a wider stitch to finish the edge.

If you have a cording foot it makes the job easier. Feed the cord through the channel farthest to the right. Also, lower the tension a bit on the top and bottom threads. If it is possible on your machine (check your manual), slightly reduce the pressure on your pressure foot.

building Boxes

The Basic Box is the place to start! Begin with a 4″ square box, follow these directions and you will be set to make any of the boxes with separate lids...from Square to Diamond. Once you have a basic box or two under your belt, you will be ready to head to the boxes with attached lids section.

What You'll Need

- **Fabric:** ½ yard of 2 fabrics (fat quarters work for some of the smaller boxes)

- **Stiff interfacing:** ⅓ yard is enough for the 4″ box (see instructions for individual boxes)

- **Fusible web:** 2 yards (1 yard is enough for some of the smaller boxes.)

- **Basic Materials** (pages 6-9)

How-To's

Cutting

1. Cut the stiff interfacing shapes required for the box you wish to make. (Refer to the individual box directions for shapes and pieces required.)

Example: A 4″ box requires stiff interfacing cut into 5 squares 4″ × 4″.

2. Use white thread to zigzag squares of stiff interfacing together with a wide, long stitch, one stitch catching each piece of stiff interfacing. Hold the pieces apart slightly as you sew. (The examples use orange thread to make the pieces easier to see. Use white thread when *you* do it!)

Example: For the 4″ box, 1 square 4″ × 4″ forms the base and 4 more squares 4″ × 4″ are attached to become the sides.

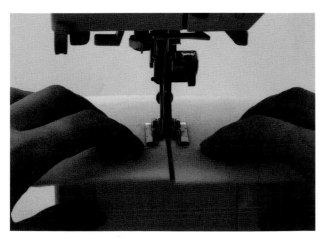

Hold the pieces apart as you sew them together.

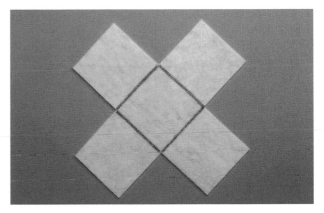

Square box base pieces sewn together

easy!

Cut your box and lid interfacing at the same time and sew both pieces with the white thread. This makes for fewer thread changes.

Fusing

1. Cut 2 fabrics and 2 layers of fusible web the size required for your box.

Example: For the 4″ box, cut the fabrics and fusible in 12½″ × 12½″ squares.

2. Fuse the web to the wrong sides of the fabric.

3. Lightly fuse 1 layer of fabric to the assembled stiff interfacing. Be sure your ironing board protective sheet is underneath the fabric and fusible when you do this.

easy!

4. Turn the piece over and trim the fabric to the outer edges of the stiff interfacing, leaving the corners square.

The fabric is ready to be trimmed.

5. Lay the second piece of fusible-backed fabric on the stiff interfacing side of the sandwich, fusible side down. Make sure it is very flat, with no wrinkles underneath. Iron the fabric onto the sandwich. Be sure to fuse the fabrics well in the corners. Iron right up to the stiff interfacing.

6. Trim the second piece of fabric even with the first piece.

Sewing the Corners

1. Fold diagonally so 2 adjacent sides of the sandwich meet with the box's interior fabrics together.

2. Match the edges of the stiff interfacing and put a pin in the excess corner fabric.

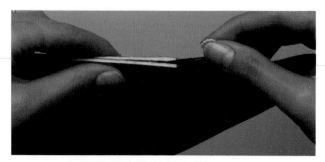

Fold the sandwich and pin for sewing.

easy!

3. Using a straight stitch, sew as close as you can along the edge of the stiff interfacing. Backstitch at the start. End the sewing about ⅛″ from the corner and backstitch. If you stop stitching before the bottom corner, the stitching will be hidden!

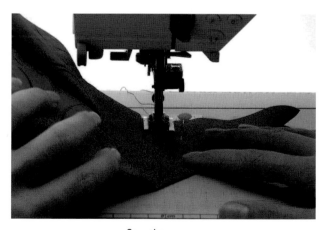

Sew the corner.

fast!

Stop stitching and backstitch about ⅛″ before the corner.

4. Continue folding and sewing the corners in the same way.

fun!

Sew the corner seams with a shortened stitch length, trim the corners off, and turn the box inside out for a finished, nonreversible box.

Finishing the Corners

1. Iron a crease in the center of the fold on each corner.

2. Bring the crease to the corner of the box and flatten the excess fabric along the sides of the box.

3. Pin the excess fabric to the box, keeping the pins below the edge. Repeat this on each corner.

Pin the excess fabric to the sides. (Pins are below the edge!)

easy!

Fold 2 corners over each other on opposite sides for a different look.

4. Steam press the corners flat against the box.

5. Trim the fabric even with the top edge of the box. Use your double-curved duck-bill appliqué scissors for an easy, clean, and even edge.

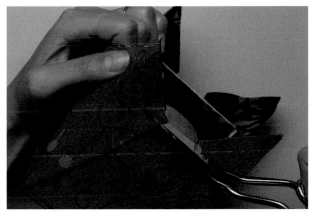

Trim the corners.

6. Fit the box over the open arm of your machine. With the cording right next to the edge of the box, zigzag it on around the edge. See Sewing the Cording, page 9.

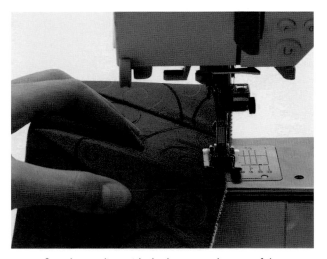

Sew the cording with the box over the arm of the sewing machine.

7. Sew around the top edge with a medium-width satin stitch. Be sure the stitch is wide enough to cover the cording and catch the edge of the box. Sew around the box again using a slightly wider satin stitch the second time around.

fast!

Use a marker to cover any threads or cording that are still showing.

Final Shaping

Set the box open-side down on your ironing board and steam press the sides and bottom flat. Don't press too hard!

easy!

A small chunk of 4 × 4 lumber with a couple of layers of cloth around it makes a great "tailor's ham" for pressing.

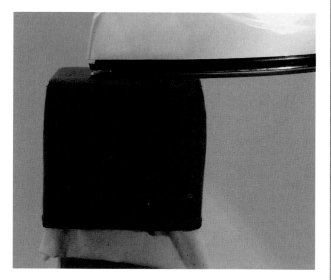

Steam the base. Using wood as a filler makes it easier.

How-To's for Lids

Cutting

1. Cut the stiff interfacing for your lid base and lid sides.

Example: For the 4″ box example, use 2 squares 4″ × 4″ for the lid sides and 1 square 4½″ × 4½″ for the lid base.

2. Draw lines across each lid side square from corner to corner. Position the piece on your cutting mat so the lines form a plus sign (pencil lines in the photo below).

3. You need to cut off 2 corners to give the lid a snug fit on the box. The width of the piece after you trim the corners will be as wide as the lid base. Place your ruler along the horizontal line, using the vertical line as the centerline of your measurement. Mark the corner trimming lines. Cut off the corners parallel to the vertical line. Repeat this on the remaining side square lid pieces.

Example: For the 4″ box, the piece after you trim the corners needs to be 4½″ trimmed corner to trimmed corner (to match the lid base). Measure along the horizontal line, centering the vertical line at 2¼″ (the center of 4½″).

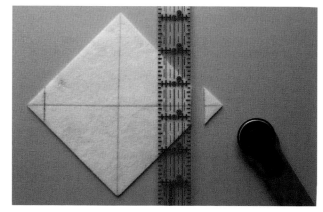

Draw 2 lines corner to corner. Nip the ends off the sides.

4. Cut both lid side squares in half along the horizontal line (through the clipped corners).

Cut on the horizontal line, trimmed edge to trimmed edge.

5. Sew these side pieces to the lid base with a loose zigzag stitch as you did for the box, holding them apart a bit as you sew.

Lid base with the side flaps sewn on

6. Cut 2 pieces of fabric and 2 pieces of fusible web ½″ larger all around.

Example: For the 4″ box, cut the fabric and web into 8″ × 8″ squares.

Fusing

1. Fuse a piece of web to the wrong side of each piece of fabric.

2. Fuse 1 piece of fabric to the assembled lid with stiff interfacing.

3. Trim the edges to match the shape of the stiff interfacing, including the little notch in the center of the sides.

4. Turn the sandwich over and fuse the other piece of fabric to the stiff interfacing.

5. Trim the edges.

Trim the lid along the stiff interfacing. Here, the second fabric is fused on and one edge is trimmed, including the notch.

Sewing the Edges

1. Zigzag cording onto the perimeter of the flat lid shape. See Sewing the Cording, page 9.

2. Satin stitch twice around the edges of the whole top while it is still flat. Use the same satin stitch widths you used on the edge of the box. Check the back side before sewing the second time around to make sure the first stitches caught all of the fabric and completely covered the edge. Don't sew around the inner corners of the notches on the side. (Sew inside the notches, just not the inside corner of it.)

Don't sew around the inner corners of the notches.

Shaping the Lid

1. Fold the corners of the lid in and press them with steam so they retain some angle.

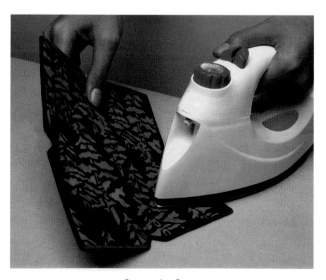

Steam the flaps.

2. The notches that become the lid corners can be sewn together by hand or machine. Fold the lid to match the corners. Sew them together with a very narrow, short-length zigzag stitch very close to the outer edge. Repeat this for each corner. Remember, you can scrunch it to get it under the needle!

Sew the lid corners.

3. Steam the flaps in a bit more as necessary if they flare out.

easy!

Set the top on the box and steam press the top flat. Press gently so you don't distort the box shape.

square Boxes

Go ahead, be square! You will think up so many variations for this one, you'll never get boxed in.

What You'll Need

- **Fabric:** 1 fat quarter of 2 fabrics for 3″ or 4″ box, ½ yard of 2 fabrics for 5″ box

- **Stiff interfacing:** ¼ yard for 3″ and 4″ box, ⅓ yard for 5″ box

- **Fusible web:** ⅝ yard for 3″ box, 1 yard for 4″ box, 1½ yards for 5″ box

- **Basic Materials** (see pages 6-9)

Square 3″ Box

Cutting

From the stiff interfacing, cut 7 squares 3″ × 3″ (5 for the box, 2 for the lid flaps) and 1 square 3½″ × 3½″ (for the lid base).

For the lid flaps, use 2 of the 3″ × 3″ stiff interfacing squares. Following the lid cutting instructions on pages 14–15, trim off the corners 1¾″ out from the center line so the trimmed corner to trimmed corner measurement is 3½″ (lid-base width).

From both fabrics, cut 1 square 10″ × 10″ for the box and 1 square 7″ × 7″ for the lid. Cut 2 of each size square from the fusible web.

Square 4″ Box

Cutting

From the stiff interfacing, cut 7 squares 4″ × 4″ (5 for the box, 2 for the lid flaps) and 1 square 4½″ × 4½″ (for the lid base).

For the lid flaps, use 2 of the 4″× 4″ stiff interfacing squares. Following the lid cutting instructions on pages 14–15, trim off the corners. Cut 2¼″ out from the drawn line, parallel with it, to match the lid base width of 4½″.

From both fabrics, cut 1 square 12½″ × 12½″ for the box and 1 square 8″× 8″ for the lid. Cut 2 of each size square from the fusible web.

Square 5″ Box

Cutting

From the stiff interfacing, cut 7 squares 5″ × 5″ (5 for the box, 2 for the lid flaps) and 1 square 5½″ × 5½″ (for the lid base).

For the lid flaps, use 2 of the 5″ × 5″ squares. Following the lid cutting instructions on pages 14–15, trim off the corners 2¾″ out from the drawn line to match the lid base width of 5½″.

From both fabrics, cut 1 square 16″× 16″ for the box and 1 square 10″ × 10″ for the lid. Cut 2 of each size square from the fusible web.

How-To's

Choose your size and cut your pieces. Refer to Building Boxes, pages 14–15, for construction.

Variations

Now comes the hard part. Figure out what to put in it and who to give it to!

Mix and match and make the boxes your own by trying some of these variations:

A. Fuse squares of a complementary fabric to the corners before stitching them closed. Box made by Sidnee Snell.

B. Match the lid fabric with the added corner squares and finish the box edges flat before sewing the corner seams. Box made by Alex Vincent.

C. Round the lid flaps and add some decorative stitching before sewing the corners of the lid. Box made by Sidnee Snell.

D. Finish the edge while the box is still flat. Fold and sew the corners on the inner side, turn it right side out, then glue mirrors on for a great jewelry box! Box made by Sidnee Snell

triangle Boxes

These three-sided treasures won't give you a tad of trouble. *Tri* a couple!

What You'll Need

- **Fabric:** ½ yard of 2 fabrics
- **Stiff interfacing:** ⅓ yard for small triangle box, ½ yard for large triangle box
- **Fusible web:** 1¾ yards for small triangle, 2 yards for large triangle box.
- **Equilateral triangle ruler (with 60° points)** (optional)
- **Basic Materials** (see pages 6-9)

Small Triangle Box

Cutting

From the stiff interfacing, cut 1 equilateral triangle 4⅛" tall (with 4¾" sides) for the box base. (Use the pattern on the pullout for the triangles if desired.) Cut 3 rectangles 4½" × 4¾" for the box sides. Cut 1 equilateral triangle 4½" tall (with 5¼" sides) for the lid base. Cut 2 squares 4½" × 4½" for the lid flaps.

Follow the lid cutting instructions on pages 14–16 to trim off the lid flaps' corners. Trim the corners 2⅝" from the center line.

easy!

> Cut only one square for the top flaps, then use one flap for a pattern for the third. No leftover piece!

From both fabrics, cut 1 rectangle 15" × 18" for the box and 1 square 9" × 9" for the lid. Cut 2 of each size from the fusible web.

Large Triangle Box

Cutting

From the stiff interfacing, cut 1 equilateral triangle 4¾" tall (with 5½" sides) for the box base. (Use the pattern on the pullout for the triangles if desired.) Cut 3 squares 5½" × 5½" for sides. Cut 1 equilateral triangle 5¼" tall (with 6⅛" sides) for the lid base. Cut 2 squares 5½" × 5½" for the lid flaps.

Follow the lid cutting instructions on pages 14–16 to trim off the lid flaps' corners 3⅟₁₆" from the center line.

From both fabrics, cut 1 rectangle 17" × 20" for the box and 1 square 11" × 11" for lid. Cut 2 of each size from the fusible web.

How-To's

Choose your size and cut your pieces. Refer to Building Boxes, pages 11–14, for construction.

Center the box lid bases on the fabrics when fusing. Remember to cut the excess base fabric away straight across the edges of the stiff interfacing. Cut to the edge of the fabric; you do not need to cut clear to a point when cutting the sides.

Align the ruler with the edge of the stiff interfacing to cut.

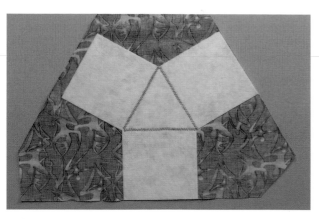

Sew the stiff interfacing together for triangle box, fuse to fabric, and trim edges. (2 edges trimmed.)

Sew the stiff interfacing together for triangle lid, fuse to fabric, and trim edges. (2 edges trimmed.)

Variations

A little bit of playing can equal a lot of fun with trusty triangle variations.

A. Add some variety by taking a square out of the lid flap to give you two (or even three) points. Box made by Sidnee Snell.

B. Cut a shaped hole in the lid flap to allow a peek of the box fabric. Box made by Sidnee Snell.

pentagon Boxes

This special little (medium or big) box will really make a hit when it's made with fabric that says something about you.

What You'll Need

- **Fabric:** 1 fat quarter of 2 fabrics for small box, ½ yard of 2 fabrics for medium or large box
- **Stiff interfacing:** ½ yard for small, medium, or large box
- **Fusible web:** 1 ½ yards for small, 2 yards for medium, 2½ yards for large (These are generous amounts.)
- **Basic Materials** (see pages 6-9)
- **Patterns on pullout**

Small Pentagon Box

Cutting

From the stiff interfacing, cut 5 squares 3″ × 3″ for box sides. Using the patterns on the pullout, cut 1 small box base, 1 small lid base, and 5 small lid flaps.

Set the sewn stiff interfacing box (or lid) on top of 2 layers of fabric and 2 layers of fusible web. Cut ½″ outside the straight edges. Be sure to leave fabric and fusible for the corners.

Medium Pentagon Box

Cutting

From the stiff interfacing, cut 5 squares 4″ × 4″ for box sides. Using the patterns on the pullout, cut 1 medium box base, 1 medium lid base, and 5 medium lid flaps.

Set the sewn stiff interfacing box (or lid) on top of 2 layers of fabric and 2 layers of fusible web. Cut ½″ outside the straight edges. Be sure to leave fabric and fusible for the corners.

Large Pentagon Box

Cutting

From the stiff interfacing, cut 5 squares 5⅛″ × 5⅛″ for box sides. Using the patterns on the pullout, cut 1 large box base, 1 large lid base, and 5 large lid flaps.

Set the sewn stiff interfacing box (or lid) on top of 2 layers of fabric and 2 layers of fusible web. Cut ½″ outside the edges. Be sure to leave fabric and fusible for the corners.

How-To's

Choose your size and cut your pieces. Refer to Building Boxes, pages 11–14, for construction.

Sew the stiff interfacing together for pentagon box, fuse to fabric, and trim edges. (3 edges trimmed.)

Sew the stiff interfacing together for pentagon lid.
(2 edges trimmed)

Trim fabric along the edges of the box.

Variations

Fabric manufacturers make it so easy to create a stack of boxes that are sure to please. Choose a theme—colorful and fun, holiday, pretty in pink, birds in flight—and have some fun.

A. Make all three sizes in coordinating fabric for nesting boxes. Boxes made by Alex Vincent.

B. Use your paper backing for a pattern and piece the lid with fused fabric to tack the seam allowances down, then add another layer of fusible web to make a smooth striking lid.

hexagon Boxes

These Hex-citing boxes can charm
the jewelry right out of your ears
or the cards right off the table!
And they make great containers
for any number of things you don't
want to lose.

What You'll Need

- **Fabric:** 1 fat quarter each of 2 fabrics for small box, ½ yard each of 2 fabrics for large box

- **Stiff interfacing:** ½ yard for small or large box

- **Fusible web:** 1½ yards for small box, 2 yards for large box

- **Basic Materials** (see pages 6-9)

- **Patterns on pullout**

Small Hexagon Box

Cutting

From the stiff interfacing, cut 6 squares $2\frac{5}{8}'' \times 2\frac{5}{8}''$ for box sides. Using the patterns on the pullout, cut 1 small box base (side edges will measure $2\frac{5}{8}''$), 1 small lid base (side edges will measure $3''$), and 6 small lid flaps.

Set the sewn stiff interfacing box (or lid) on top of 2 layers of fabric and 2 layers of fusible web. Cut ½" outside the straight edges. Be sure to leave fabric and fusible for the corners of the box.

Large Hexagon Box

Cutting

From the stiff interfacing, cut 6 squares $3\frac{3}{4}'' \times 3\frac{3}{4}''$ for box sides. Using the patterns on the pullout, cut 1 large box base (side edges will measure $3\frac{3}{4}''$), 1 large lid base (side edges will measure $4\frac{1}{8}''$), and 6 large lid flaps.

Set the sewn stiff interfacing box (or lid) on top of 2 layers of fabric and 2 layers of fusible web. Cut ½" outside the straight edges. Be sure to leave fabric and fusible for the corners of the box.

How-To's

Choose your size and cut your pieces. Refer to Building Boxes, pages 11-14, for construction.

Sew the stiff interfacing together for hexagon box, fuse to fabric, and trim edges. (4 edges trimmed.)

Sew the stiff interfacing together for hexagon lid, fuse to fabric, and trim edges and notches. (3 edges trimmed.)

fun!

Use the top of one of your boxes to display all your quilt guild, quilt shop, and workshop pins.

Variations

These delicate shaped boxes can store everyday items or special treasures. Be sure to make one just the right size for your own unique needs.

A. Curve the lid flaps in and out and add some beads for a unique gift box. Box made by Kim Campbell.

B. Fuse fabric to stiff interfacing cut the right size and you can make some great divisions to keep your treasures separated. Box made by Sidnee Snell.

C. Streeetch up those sides and make it the right size to hold a container of hand wipes for the car or the baby's room. You can even nip the corners of the base just a bit to make a 12-sided box and play with the folds like Libby Ankarberg.

diamond Box

For a jewel of a box, try this diamond box. It's sure to catch everyone's eyes and make them sparkle.

What You'll Need

- ☐ **Fabric:** ½ yard of 2 fabrics
- ☐ **Stiff interfacing:** ½ yard
- ☐ **Fusible web:** 1½ yards
- ☐ **Ruler with marked 30°/60° lines** (optional)
- ☐ **Basic Materials** (see pages 6-9)

Cutting

From stiff interfacing, cut a 60° diamond 3½" wide for box base, using the pattern on the pull-out. Cut 4 rectangles 4" × 4¾" for sides. Cut a 60° diamond 4" wide for the lid base, using the pattern on the pullout. Cut 2 rectangles 5¾" × 2¾" for the lid flaps.

To trim the lid flaps, cut the rectangles in half diagonally. Mark 4⅝" on the long straight edge (not the diagonal edge) of the triangle and nip the corners parallel to the 2¾" side of the triangle. The length of the straight side of the piece should match the side of the diamond top.

Cut 1 fabric rectangle 16" × 18" for the box and 1 fabric square 11" × 11" for the lid from both fabrics. Cut 2 of each shape from the fusible web.

How-To's

Choose your size and cut your pieces. Refer to Building Boxes, pages 11–14, for construction.

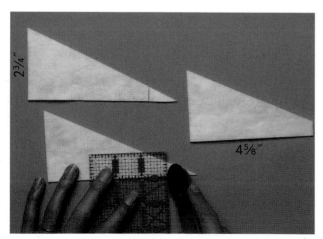

Cut the flaps for the diamond box lid.

Sew the stiff interfacing together for the diamond box, fuse to fabric, and trim edges. (2 edges trimmed.)

Sew the stiff interfacing together for the diamond lid, fuse to fabric, and trim edges. (3 edges trimmed.)

When the lid is fused and trimmed, fold it inside out, match the edges of the stiff interfacing, and sew the corners as you do for the boxes. Trim these seams to ⅛" and turn the lid right side out. Finish the edges with satin stitching. You can use some fray check, fray block, or thread fuse on the seam *after* you've done the satin stitching. If you do this before stitching, it dries to a plastic and you will break needles!

easy!

Cut your box fabric too short for the corners? Just sew the corners with a shorter stitch length, trim them to about ⅛″ from the box, and reverse the box.

fun!

Don't want to satin stitch? Fuse and trim the inside fabric. Cut the outside fabric for your box about ½″ to ¾″ wider on each side. Fold the edges over and fuse them down before sewing the corners. Sew the corners to the inside and trim them to about ⅛″. Turn the box right side out. Voilà, no satin stitching!

Variations

Diamonds are forever, so make one for your best friend and play a little to make sure she knows it's from you.

A. Try changing the height of the sides and use the fabric motif on the inside fabric to do some bobbin embroidery before you sew up the sides.

B. Piece the fabric for the top, and if you're tired of satin stitching, add some prairie points to the edge of the box. Box made by Alex Vincent.

recipe Box with attached lid

Whip up this box for an afternoon snack, put some treats in it to munch…What a recipe for fun!

What You'll Need

☐ **Fabric:** 1 fat quarter of 2 fabrics

☐ **Stif interfacing:** ⅓ yard

☐ **Fusible web:** 1½ yards fusible web

☐ **90/14 topstitch needles**

☐ **Basic Materials** (see page 6-9)

This box will require more crunching of the stiff interfacing. Just pin it well while you are sewing and it will steam back to shape beautifully. Start with the 4″ square box with an attatched lid to learn the technique, and then have fun with some rectangluar variations.

Square 4″ Box

Cutting

From stiff interfacing, cut 5 squares 4″ × 4″ for box base and sides. Cut 1 rectangle 4¼″ × 4⅛″ for lid base. Cut 1 rectangle 2″ × 4¼″ for lid front. Cut 2 rectangles 2″ × 4⅛″ for lid side.

Cut 1 corner off each lid side rectangle at a 45° angle.

Cut 1 rectangle 13″ × 19″ from both fabrics. Cut 2 rectangles 13″ × 19″ from fusible web.

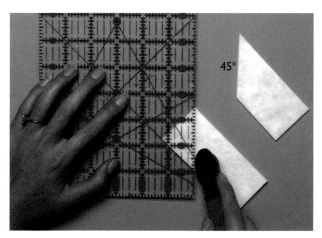

Cut the corner off the top flap.

Small Recipe Box

Cutting

From stiff interfacing, cut 1 rectangle 3½″ × 5½″ for box base. Cut 2 squares 3½″ × 3½″ for box ends. Cut 2 rectangles 3½″ × 5½″ for box sides. Cut 1 rectangle 3¾″ × 5¾″ for lid base. Cut 2 rectangles 1½″ × 3¾″ for lid sides. Cut 1 rectangle 1½″ × 5¾″ for lid front.

Cut 1 corner off each lid side rectangle at a 45° angle.

Cut 1 rectangle 13″ × 18″ from both fabrics. Cut 2 rectangles 13″ × 18″ from fusible web.

Large Recipe Box

Cutting

From stiff interfacing, cut 1 rectangle 4¼″ × 6½″ for box base. Cut 2 rectangles 4¼″ × 4½″ for box ends. Cut 2 rectangles 4½″ × 6½″ for box sides. Cut 1 rectangle 4½″ × 6¾″ for lid base. Cut 2 rectangles 2″ × 4½″ for lid sides. Cut 1 rectangle 2″ × 6¾″ for lid front.

Cut 1 corner off each lid side rectangle at a 45° angle.

Cut 1 rectangle 16″ × 20″ from both fabrics. Cut 2 rectangles 16″ × 20″ from fusible web.

How-To's

Choose your size and cut your pieces. Refer to Building Boxes, pages 14–15, for construction.

Sewing the Stiff Interfacing

1. Zigzag the box sides and ends to the base piece, holding the pieces apart gently as you sew.

2. Zigzag the front and sides to the lid.

3. Center the remaining edge of the lid to the box (⅛″ over on each end), and zigzag the lid to the box.

Fusing the Fabrics

1. Lay the box shape on top of your fabric and fusible web and cut generously around it with a rotary cutter and ruler. Be sure to leave fabric and fusible for the corners.

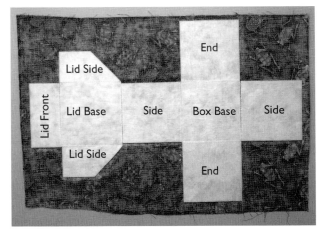

Sew the stiff interfacing together and center over fabric and fusible.

2. Fuse the web to the back sides of the fabric.

easy!

Keep the paper backing from the first side of fusible underneath when you iron on the second piece. Then you won't have to clean up fusible after ironing—it will still be on your fabric!

3. Fuse 1 layer of fabric to the stiff interfacing shape. Be sure you have the ironing board protective sheet underneath!

4. On the box portion only, use the sides of the stiff interfacing as the outside edge, and cut straight across with a ruler. On the side next to the lid, cut only to the stiff interfacing lid piece.

5. Next, use the sides of the lid and cut the outer edge the same way.

6. Trim along the 45° angle of the lid edges.

Trim the box and lid bottom.

7. With the stiff interfacing side down, center the box on your second fabric. Carefully turn it all over. Make sure it is very flat, with no wrinkles underneath. Press the sandwich together with an iron just enough to hold the new piece of fabric in place, then flip the sandwich and trim it.

8. Once again, make sure there are no wrinkles and fuse the fabric well on both sides. Be sure to press the iron well into the "corners" where the fabric meets fabric.

Shaping

1. Fold the box diagonally, match the corners of the stiff interfacing, and iron a crease in the center of the fold on 1 corner.

2. Bring the creased fabric across the box and flatten the excess fabric along the sides of the box.

3. Pin this corner fabric to the side of the box, keeping the pins below the edge.

4. Pin all 4 corners in the same way, overlapping the excess fabric to the sides of the box.

5. Pin the 2 corners of the lid in the same way.

Pin the box sides well before sewing the edge.

Pin the lid corners to the sides.

fun!

Play a little to see which side you want to cross over the other. You can even embellish these corner overlaps!

easy!

Use quilter's flat flower pins. They are more flexible, bend a bit as you go around the corners, and can still be bent back to shape easily.

Finishing

1. Steam press the corners flat against the box.

2. Trim the fabric even with the top edge of the box. Use your double-curved duck-bill embroidery scissors to get the edge nice and even.

3. Zigzag a length of cording around the edge, then sew the unfinished edges twice around with a medium-width satin stitch. Use a slightly wider stitch the second time around. You will need to work a bit on the corners to keep the stiff interfacing edges close together.

4. Start with the box part over the arm of your sewing machine. Turn the corners of the lid inside out to sew continuously around the edge.

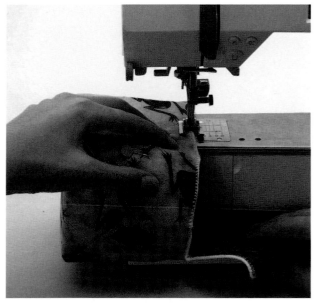

Place the box portion over your sewing machine arm.

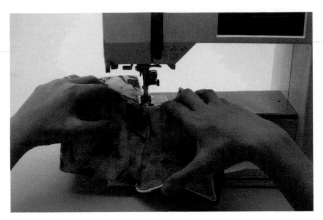

5. Steam press the bottom and top flat, and steam the side flaps in a bit.

Fill the box with copies of your recipe cards and pass on an heirloom.

Turn the lid inside out to satin stitch a continuous line.

Variations

Want to see your gift in use when you go to a friend's house? The right fabric can make this box a surefire recipe for success.

A. Finish the lid edges before sewing and give your box some "ears" to go with the fabric on a large square Recipe Box.

B. This one's for the soccer kid. The lid edges were contoured to the soccer balls on the fabric.

C. Made especially for the chili or Southwestern fan, this is one recipe box that won't get hidden in the cupboard!

A

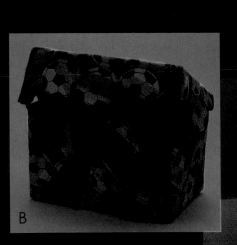

B

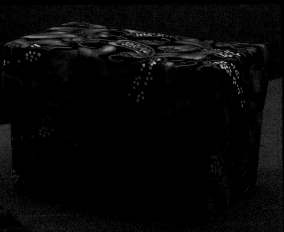

C

treasure Box

Want to give a real treasure to a special friend? Use some ornate fabrics and this box will inspire you to luscious heights! You can hide the gift inside, or make the box the gift. When choosing fabric, consider silk. It works well here! You may need to interface it first if it is lightweight, and use a lower iron temperature.

What You'll Need

- ☐ **Fabric:** 1 fat quarter of 2 fabrics
- ☐ **Stiff interfacing:** ⅓ yard
- ☐ **Fusible web:** ⅔ yard for small box, 1 yard for large box
- ☐ **Basic Materials** (see pages 6-9)
- ☐ **Patterns on pullout for lid ends**

3″ × 5″ Treasure Box
Cutting

From stiff interfacing, cut 3 rectangles 3″ × 5″ for box base and sides. Cut 2 squares 3″ × 3″ for box ends. Cut 1 rectangle 5″ × 6¾″ for lid base. Trim 1 end of the lid to a point, starting 2½″ in from the end. Using the pattern on the pullout, cut out 2 lid ends (base length 3″).

Cut 1 rectangle 10″ × 12″ from both fabrics. Cut 2 rectangles 10″ × 12″ from fusible web. Lid pieces will be individually trimmed when the first fabric is fused on. (Lid and box are fused separately.)

4″ × 6″ Treasure Box
Cutting

From stiff interfacing, cut 3 rectangles 4″ × 6″ for box base and sides. Cut 2 squares 4″ × 4″ for box ends. Cut 1 piece 6″ × 9½″ for lid base. Trim 1 end to a point, starting 3″ in from the end. Using the pattern on the pullout, cut out 2 lid ends (base length 4″).

Cut 1 rectangle 13″ × 15″ from both fabrics. Cut 2 rectangles 13″ × 15″ from fusible web. Lid pieces will be individually trimmed when the first fabric is fused on.

How-To's

Choose your size and cut your pieces. Refer to Building Boxes, pages 11-14 for fusing instructions for the box. The stiff interfacing for the box (not the lid) is sewn together and trimmed like the square box, page 12, with the squares sewn onto either side of the middle rectangle.

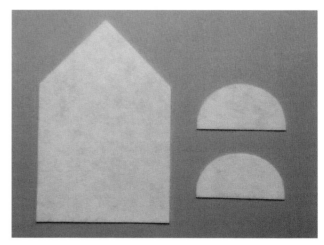

Cut the stiff interfacing for the lid pieces (including cutting 45° corners off the lid base). They will be fused separately.

Shaping

1. On the inside fabric of your box, iron firmly between the pieces of stiff interfacing where the 2 fabrics fuse to each other. This makes a visible crease line to follow when you sew the corners.

Iron firmly into the "corners."

2. Fold the box diagonally, with the *inside out.* Match the corners so the adjacent sides of stiff interfacing are parallel.

Match the edges of the box before you sew the corners.

3. Shorten your stitch length and sew as close as possible right along the edge of the stiff interfacing. Backstitch at the start and end.

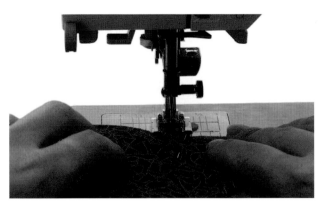

Sew as close as possible to the edge of the box.

4. With sharp scissors, trim away the excess fabric on the corners. Leave about ⅛″.

5. Zigzag a length of cording around the top edge of the box, then turn the box right side out and steam press to shape.

Finishing

With the box right side out, satin stitch twice around the edge of the box.

Making the Lid

1. Fuse both fabrics to the top pieces individually. Trim fabric to the stiff interfacing shape before fusing on the second fabric. When fusing your fabric to the curved top, fuse the inside a half at a time and use your iron to make the piece curve.

2. Curve the piece the other way over the edge of your ironing board to iron on the second piece of fabric. This reduces wrinkles in the top of the box.

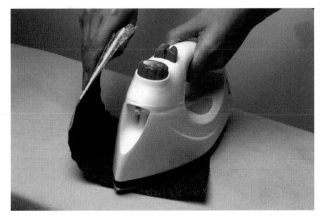

Iron a concave curve into the top as you fuse the inside fabric on.

Iron a convex curve into the top as you fuse the outside fabric on.

3. Satin stitch the edges on each of the top pieces separately.

4. Use a mending stitch or narrow zigzag stitch to sew the rounded end pieces onto the lid top. Begin stitching on each end piece from the same side of the lid. This means that you would sew 1 side on with the lid inside out.

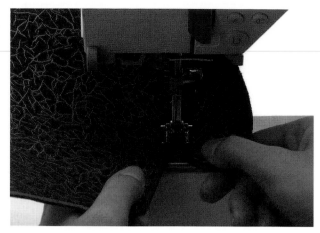

Sew the rounded ends onto the top.

Joining Lid and Box

Slide both the top and the box under the machine and sew them together along the back of the box, with a mending stitch. You may not be able to sew from corner to corner. That's okay; this is just a hinge. You can even sew it in just 2 or 3 places to make it look more like a hinge.

This is one "treasure" you won't want to hide!

Variations

A Treasure Box can hold anything your heart desires. Dress it up for show or down for function, or even change the basic shape. It can go anywhere.

A. Create a Triangle Box and attach the lid the same way you did for the Treasure Box. Anything is possible! Box made by Sidnee Snell.

B. With straps of faux suede glued on and a bevy of treasure inside, this Treasure Box would make any little girl happy for hours. Box made by Libby Ankarberg.

B

A

to go Box

What a fun way to take your lunch to work! Unwrap the ribbons to lay the box out flat for a lunch cloth; remember, it's washable. (Prewash your fabric so it won't shrink once it's constructed.) Make it with heat-resistant cloth and it will even keep your food warm.

What You'll Need

- **Fabric:** 1 fat quarter of 2 fabrics for smaller boxes, ⅝ yard for large boxes
- **Stiff interfacing:** ¾ yard
- **Fusible web:** 1 yard, 1½ yards for large
- **15″ square rotary ruler** (12½″ square ruler works for the small box)
- **Accessories:** Thin cording or size 3 crochet thread

- **3 buttons or 3 small hinch/hair pins** if you don't want to sew on buttons with shanks, or want to be able to remove buttons for washing (see Sources)
- **1 yard ribbon or string** for the ties
- **Basic Materials** (see pages 6-9)
- **Patterns on the pullout**
- **Optional:** Overcasting or cording foot for your machine

Cutting

Use the patterns on the pullout to cut stiff interfacing for the 2 box sides, 2 box ends, 1 box base, 2 side flaps, and 2 end flaps.

Set the sewn stiff interfacing box pieces on top of 2 layers of fabric and 2 layers of fusible web. Cut a square ½″ beyond the edges.

Cut the ribbon or string in thirds.

How-To's

Choose a size and cut stiff interfacing and fabric.

Sew the stiff interfacing pieces together as shown. Use a wide, long zigzag stitch and hold the pieces gently apart as you sew.

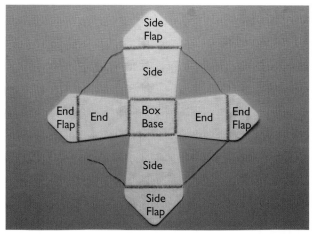

Sew the stiff interfacing together for the To Go box.

Making the Sandwich

1. Iron the fusible web to the back sides of the fabric.

2. Fuse 1 layer of fabric to the stiff interfacing "cross."

3. Trim the fabric to a square, using the sides of the stiff interfacing as the outside edge.

"Cross" with fabric fused and all edges trimmed. Trim each side after fusing it on. Photo also shows cutout described in Step 4.

4. Make a template of Cut Out Piece pattern on the pullout and place it with the shortest side right beside the stiff interfacing at the side and end flaps. Cut out the small triangle on both sides of each flap. This requires reversing the template on 1 side of each lid flap.

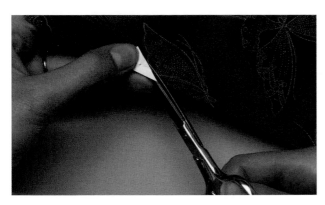

Use "Cut Out Piece" to trim edge.

5. With a pressing sheet underneath, lay the second piece of fusible-backed fabric, fusible side down, on the reverse side of the sandwich. Make sure it is very flat, with no wrinkles underneath. Iron the fabric on to the sandwich. Be sure to fuse the 2 fabrics on the corners well (with no stiff interfacing between them). Press the iron right up to the edge of the stiff interfacing.

6. Trim the second piece of fabric the same as the first, including the cut out.

7. Zigzag cording around the edge.

Shaping

1. Bring 2 sides of the box together and match the edges of the stiff interfacing on 1 end. Pin just off the edge of the stiff interfacing. Iron a crease in the fused fabric.

Pin the corner, then iron a crease.

2. Fold and crease all the corners in the same way.

3. Overlap the corners at the ends and pin them together to hold the box.

4. Mark a spot on the outside fold, ½″ in from the fold, for the button. Mark another spot on the underneath fold, about 1″ away from the first spot, for ribbon placement.

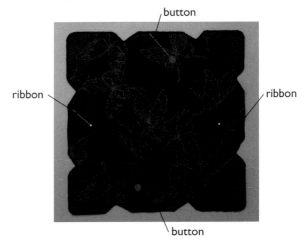

Use pins to mark the placement for the ribbons and buttons.

fun!

Before placing the buttons and ribbons, play a bit to find which way you want to fold the corners, which flaps you want in first, and how you want the fasteners to work.

5. Fold in the lid side flaps. Fold in the lid end flaps over the side flaps and mark each one about ½″ from the edges that meet. This will be the placement for your button and ribbon on the top. Wrapping the ribbon or string around the button will hold the box together while carrying things in it.

6. Unpin the box corners and sew on the buttons and ribbons where they are marked.

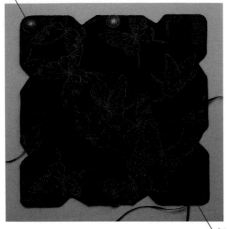

top button

top ribbon

Buttons and ribbons are ready to tie this up.

In traditional To Go boxes, the side flaps fold in last, but I find that folding the side flaps in first works better to keep the box square while traveling.

Fold it up, fill it up, and go to lunch!

Fortune Cookie Coasters

Cookies steam iron open to become coasters.

What You'll Need

- ☐ **Fabric:** 1 square 4″ × 4″ (or 4″ circle) of 2 fabrics for each coaster
- ☐ **Stiff interfacing:** 1 square 4″ × 4″ (or 4″ circle) for each coaster
- ☐ **Fusible web:** 2 squares 4″ × 4″ (or 4″ circle) for each coaster
- ☐ **Basic Materials** (see pages 6-9)

How-To's

Choose your fabric and cut out the pieces. You can cut them as 1 big piece or 6 to 8 small squares. (An 8″ × 16″ piece of fabric yields 8 coasters.)

Making the Coasters

1. Iron the fusible to the back of the fabrics.

2. Fuse the fabrics to each side of the stiff interfacing.

3. Mark and cut 3½″ circles.

easy!

Use a circle rotary cutter and set it for 3½″ circles. (Radius will be 1¾″.)

4. Satin stitch around the edges, using cording or not as you choose.

5. To shape to a fortune cookie, steam iron the coaster. You can spray it with a bit of water before you steam iron to add more flexibility.

6. While it is still warm, pull 2 opposite sides together. Hold them together while you pull the folded ends back toward each other. Pin these edges together and let the cookie bake (dry!).

First fold: Pull 2 opposite sides together.

Pull folded edges back to meet.

Variations

Whether you are taking a lunch, going on a picnic, or giving a gift, these sweet boxes will carry the day.

A. Shiny gold Christmas tablecloth fabric makes this To Go Box ready to hold a gift or food treat for that special someone.

B. A subtle tan batik and matching leather ties create a calmer mood for this To Go Box.

C. Fill up a Valentine To Go Box with chocolates and sweet fortune cookie messages, and your sweetheart won't be able to resist. Two buttons on top keep this one closed.

D. Fuse or sew a binding around the edge and add handles to this lower, wider variation and you have a great way to do take out—with some frogs to accompany you! I used stretchy wrapping cord for closures on this box.

E. Bandana box and coasters. Fix a big picnic for your favorite cowboy – and be sure to make a BIG handkerchief To Go Box with matching coasters & napkins.

fun with
embellishments

Now that you've made a few boxes, it's TIME TO PLAY! Add your own personality to any of the boxes. Find some fun yarns, buttons, beads, and tassels and let your creativity run free.

A. Beaded Fringe Trim the top with beads. You don't even have to make it yourself! Check craft and fabric stores for premade trim. Box made by Kim Campbell, embellishment by Linda.

B. Buttons Fuse on some different fabric for the corners and add a coordinating large button to serve as a handle or decoration. Box made by Alex Vincent.

C. Earrings and Fabric Linda used her own hand-dyed fabric, purchased wood grain fabric, and clipped the ends off earring posts to embellish this treasure of a steamer trunk.

D. Bobbin Stitching Some heavy decorative thread in the bobbin and tracings from a large floral fabric on the inside were combined to create the bobbin embellishment for this Diamond Box.

E. **Small Mirrors** After stitching on the lid, mirrors were glued on to brighten up this fun jewelry box. Box made by Sidnee Snell.

F. **Prairie Points** Fused on square prairie points finish the box edge and strips of different fabrics decorate the top of this Diamond Box. Box made by Alex Vincent.

G. **Ribbons** This Christmas "present" was finished with bound edges and the trim glued on. Check your trim for temperature sensitivity or shape first. Box made by Libby Ankarberg.

H. **Beads and Tassels** Beads on top, a decorative line of stitching, and some tassels dress this box up. Box made by Sidnee Snell.

About the Author

Evan Thatcher

Linda Johansen, author of *Fast, Fun & Easy Fabric Bowls*, lives in Corvallis, Oregon. She and her husband love it there because they are about two hours from the mountains, the high desert, the beach, and Portland or Eugene, without having to live there. She now teaches quilting, fabric dyeing, and how to make fabric bowls and boxes. In other lives, she has taught ballroom dancing and dog obedience.

Linda has been sewing and playing with fabric for most of her life. Her fascination with quilting comes from the endless possibilities and the variety of techniques available to anyone, no matter what his or her quilting interests. She is most fond of projects where there are no rules. Linda is currently working on her third book in the Fast, Fun & Easy series; watch for more fun coming your way!

Sources

For materials and tools mentioned in this book, check your local quilt shop.

fast2fuse™ INTERFACING:
Double-Sided Fusible Stiff Interfacing

C&T Publishing
1-800-284-1114
www.ctpub.com

Double-Sided Fusible Stiff Interfacing

Prym-Dritz Corporation
P.O. Box 5028
Spartanburg, SC 29304
www.dritz.com

Available at your local chain store

Timtex™: 22" wide yardage; a bolt holds 10 yards

Timber Lane Press (Timtex™ is made exclusively for this company; will take wholesale orders or recommend retail outlets)

24350 N. Rimrock Road
Hayden, ID 83835
(208) 765-3353
(800) 752-3353 wholesale orders only
Email: qltblox@earthlink.net

Also available through major quilting supply distributors and your local quilt shop

Isacord Thread

OESD - Oklahoma Embroidery Supply & Design

embroideryonline.com
Or ask your favorite quilt store to carry it! Large spools carry 1,000 meters. The small spools are sold as Mettler Polysheen, with 200 meters.

Pellon: Wonder Under Transfer
Web #805

Available at most Quilt and Sewing stores.
Or contact Freudenberg - Pellon
1-800-331-6509

Size 16 (¹⁄₁₆") Polyester Cording

Craft stores and general fabric stores. Wholesale through Checkers or Peterson-Arne (look for Conso or Hollywood Trim)

Hand-dyed fabrics

Johansen Dyeworks (hand-dyed fabrics)

465 SE Bridgeway Ave.
Corvallis, OR 97333
(541) 758 - 9333
Email: lindajo@peak.org
Web site: www.lindajohansen.com

Additional Supplies

Quilting Supplies

Cotton Patch Mail Order

3405 Hall Lane, Dept. CTB
Lafayette, CA 94549
Phone: 1-800-835-4418
Email: quiltusa@yahoo.com
Web: www.quiltusa.com

A Common Thread (stiff interfacing yardage, Clearview Triangle, and other assorted tools and fabrics)

16925 SW 65th
Lake Oswego, OR 97035
(877) 915–6789 (toll free)
Email: actbernina@aol.com
Web site: www.acommonthreadfabrics.com